GREAT MINDS
of Ancient Science and Math

THE GREATEST DOCTOR OF ANCIENT TIMES

HIPPOCRATES AND HIS OATH

Mary Gow

Enslow Publishers, Inc.

Library of Congress Cataloging-in-Publication Data

Gow, Mary.
   The greatest doctor of ancient times : Hippocrates and his oath / Mary Gow.
      p. cm. — (Great minds of ancient science and math)
   Summary: "A biography of ancient Greek physician Hippocrates, the Father of Medicine. His assumptions that diseases and cures came from nature, not the gods, and that a physician could treat a patient using knowledge obtained from experience or medical texts still form the basis of modern medicine"—Provided by publisher.
   Includes bibliographical references and index.
   ISBN-13: 978-0-7660-3118-0
   ISBN-10: 0-7660-3118-7
   1. Hippocrates—Juvenile literature. 2. Medicine, Greek and Roman—Juvenile literature. 3. Physicians—Biography—Juvenile literature. I. Title.
      R126.H8G556 2010
      610.938—dc22
                                        2008029630

Printed in the United States of America

10 9 8 7 6 5 4 3 2 1

To Our Readers: We have done our best to make sure all Internet addresses in this book were active and appropriate when we went to press. However, the author and the publisher have no control over and assume no liability for the material available on those Internet sites or on other Web sites they may link to. Any comments or suggestions can be sent by e-mail to comments@enslow.com or to the address on the back cover.

♻ Enslow Publishers, Inc., is committed to printing our books on recycled paper. The paper in every book contains 10% to 30% post-consumer waste (PCW). The cover board on the outside of each book contains 100% PCW. Our goal is to do our part to help young people and the environment too!

CONTENTS

1

"The Divine Hippocrates"

TO LEARN ABOUT AN ILLNESS OR HEALTH condition today, you may start your inquiry at your school or local library. In one section, you will find books on a variety of medical and health subjects. Books about conditions, such as asthma, AIDS, diabetes, and infectious diseases, such as rabies, the common cold, and tuberculosis are likely there. Some titles may address eating disorders, sports medicine, or women's health. Common surgeries are explained in some, others describe healing therapies. The books on your library shelves were written by different authors. They present the science of different ailments, discuss ways to stay healthy, and describe treatment and care of patients.

Now, turn the clock back about two thousand years and imagine yourself in an ancient Greek library. Perhaps you are at the great library of Alexandria or the library of Pergamum. These libraries look different from their modern counterparts. Instead of today's familiar books with rectangular covers and bound pages with printed words, ancient Greek libraries first had collections of texts handwritten on papyrus. Papyrus is a paperlike material made from reeds. Papyrus rolls, some more than ten feet long, were kept in pottery or leather cases on library shelves. The library in Alexandria, a Greek city in northern Egypt, had more than 490,000 papyrus rolls in its collection during the third century (299–200) B.C. The library of Pergamum in Asia Minor, now in the country of Turkey, reportedly had more than two hundred thousand rolls.

In your imaginary visit to one of these ancient libraries, suppose you again are interested in medical books. Scholars there would likely direct you to a respected collection of texts. Within this collection are many medical writings. These texts deal with ailments, such as pneumonia and malaria. Some have guidelines for setting bones and bandaging wounds. Stomachaches, headaches, childbirth, and eye afflictions are addressed. Some books deal with regimen—diet and exercise. Physicians' duties and professional conduct are among their subjects. These books were written in a time when people believed in gods and goddesses with superhuman powers, but none of the texts rely on magical or superstitious treatments.

"I will use my power to help the sick to the best of my ability and judgment; I will abstain from harming or wronging any man by it," is stated in the most famous work in the collection.[1] This text, the *Hippocratic Oath,* lays out a code of conduct for physicians, outlining their expected behavior and responsibilities.

Principles for examining patients are clearly described in a text titled *Prognosis.* Observing signs, such as fever, the patient's appearance, and points of discomfort are emphasized. *Regimen for*

No portraits of Hippocrates from his lifetime exist today. This 1638 engraving by Peter Paul Rubens is the artist's idea of the ancient physician's possible appearance.

Acute Diseases presents treatments for ailments including pneumonia. Some volumes show the Greeks' emerging theory of balance of bodily fluids, called humors. One scrapbook-like volume offers snippets of medical wisdom. "Desperate cases need the most desperate remedies," says one.[2] "Hard work is undesirable for the underfed," reads another.[3] Reading these texts, one can hear these compassionate doctors still speaking to us across the centuries.

Some volumes provide a direct look at patients. "Crito in Thasos had a violent pain in the foot which came on while walking; it started from the big toe," opens one entry in a text titled *Epidemics*. "The same day he took to his bed with shivering nausea and slight fever; at night he became delirious." The patient's further signs are briefly described. Crito, the author noted, "died on the second day."[4]

This collection of medical works was written by many different writers. Most of its authors were physicians, a few were teachers. The majority of the texts date from 430 to 330 B.C.[5] Textbooks for physicians, lectures for general audiences about medical subjects, and practical manuals with straightforward instructions are among them. This body of writing is known as the Hippocratic Collection or the Hippocratic Corpus. *Corpus* is the Latin word meaning "body."

These are the earliest existing documents written by doctors themselves that show how they saw their profession. About sixty Hippocratic writings from ancient Greece exist today. The *Hippocratic Oath* is among them. In the United States, most doctors pledge an oath derived from this ancient promise. This oath and these writings carry the name of an ancient Greek physician, Hippocrates.

We do not know where the Hippocratic Collection was first assembled, but by 250 B.C. some of its texts were studied by physicians in the Greek city of Alexandria, Egypt. Scholars at the Museum there, an ancient university, read Hippocratic writings. They wrote commentaries about the texts and even glossaries of their medical words.[6] The theories and practices in these texts became prominent in the ancient world.

The Hippocratic writings laid the foundations for Western scientific medicine.[7] In them, we see the Greeks' investigations into causes of diseases. They express the Greek view that humankind was a part of the natural world. Belonging to the natural world, humankind was seen to be made up of the substances of the world and to be subject to laws of cause and effect.[8] The Hippocratic writers did not blame gods and goddesses for sickness, and they did not expect them to restore health. One text attacks practitioners who claimed that charms and incantations could heal the ill. The

Hippocratic author called those men frauds and charlatans.

Since that distant age in ancient Alexandria, these writings have been tied to the name Hippocrates. Hippocrates was long seen as the ideal physician—knowledgeable, caring, and skilled. Along with being a doctor and teacher of medicine, Hippocrates was considered the author of at least some of the Hippocratic texts.

Problems With Hippocrates

There are challenges in studying any person from the distant past. Many texts from ancient Greece have survived the centuries. These include histories, philosophical writings, plays, and poems. Archaeologists have excavated temples, neighborhoods, city centers, and villages. Ruins and artifacts have revealed much about the ancient Greek people and their culture. Although we know a lot about the Greek world, many questions remain.

Traditionally, Hippocrates is said to have been born about 460 B.C. and to have died about

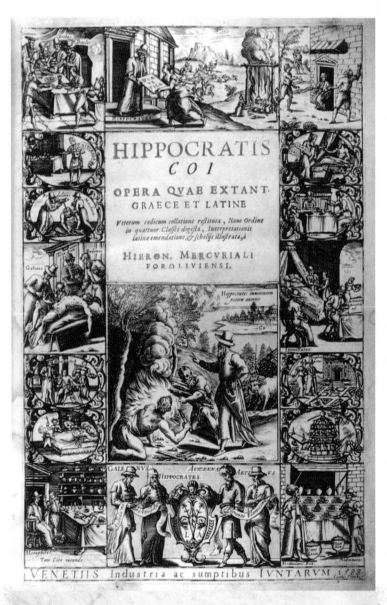

This engraving was the title page of a 1588 volume of writings attributed to Hippocrates of Cos. Its individual medical scenes show Hippocrates and other ancient doctors at work.

380 B.C. His home was always identified as the island of Cos. Considering Hippocrates' great fame in the ancient world, at first glance it appears that much is known about this famous physician. Closer examination, though, shows a different story.

Two references in the writings of Plato, the philosopher, point the way to Hippocrates. Plato lived from about 427 to 347 B.C. Founder of the Academy (a school in Athens), Plato wrote many philosophical works. In his writings, Plato referred to a doctor named Hippocrates from Cos. Aristotle, another great philosopher, who lived a little later, about 384 to 322 B.C., also mentioned Hippocrates as a famous doctor.

From the writings of Alexandrian doctors, we know that Hippocratic texts were being studied in 250 B.C. We do not know which specific texts they had at that time. By the end of that century, stories about Hippocrates were told and repeated.[9] Some of these accounts may have been grounded in truth. Others were fiction.

Letters, two speeches, and even an Athenian decree relating to Hippocrates, the doctor,

13

became attached to the medical texts. They portray Hippocrates as a patriot loyal to his homeland, a wise and honorable man, and a skilled versatile physician. These letters, speeches, and the decree are examples of *pseudepigraphy*, which means "falsely inscribed."[10] Ancient Greeks had a tradition of composing imaginary letters and speeches about famous people, sometimes even as school exercises.[11] The pseudepigraphy are all considered fiction. Unfortunately, their vivid accounts of Hippocrates curing a plague, diagnosing a lovesick king, and as a Greek patriot do not tell us anything about the real doctor from Cos.

Fictional stories about famous people are not unique to the Greeks. In the stories about Hippocrates, he was shown embodying qualities that Greeks admired. The tales showed his wisdom, his patriotism, and his cleverness. In American history, we can find similar accounts. One well-known example about George Washington was taught in schoolbooks for decades. It was intended to illustrate the first

Dating from the late second to first century B.C. this fragment of papyrus was discovered in Egypt. The Greek writing on it is a section of the Hippocratic text titled *Epidemics*.

president's early love of truth. As a young boy, George was supposedly given a little hatchet, which he soon applied to one of his father's prized cherry trees. When his father questioned him about the damaged tree, George honestly confessed his deed. He was not punished because his father valued honesty more than the tree. This fictional account first appeared in a popular book written by Mason Locke Weems that was published a few years after Washington died.

There is no question that Hippocrates' reputation was great in the ancient world. Paetus, a first century Roman senator and philosopher, called the ancient Greek "The divine Hippocrates."[12] The Roman philosopher Seneca called him "The greatest physician."[13] "Let us begin with the words of Hippocrates as with a voice from a god," wrote Galen.[14] Greek by birth and a citizen of the Roman Empire, Galen was a physician and a prolific medical writer. Much of his own groundbreaking medical work was built on Hippocratic ideas. Galen, Seneca, Paetus, and other ancients knew that Hippocrates was not the author of all of the texts in the collection. But they believed that he wrote some of them.

Hippocrates' reputation stood up for centuries. Hippocratic texts were translated into Arabic and studied in the Islamic world during the European Middle Ages. They were rediscovered again in Europe during the Renaissance, in the fifteenth and sixteenth centuries, and influenced a new age of medical thought. Hippocrates, the man and the doctor, was widely admired.

In recent years, scholars have been less accepting of the traditional picture of historic Hippocrates and his connection to these texts. One classical scholar, Ulrich von Wilamowitz-Moellendorf, claimed that Hippocrates was "a famous name without the background of a single treatise."[15] Another scholar, Ludwig Edelstein, asserted that Hippocrates is "a name lacking even any accessible historical reality."[16]

In studying Hippocrates today, we do not find a neat package of facts about one man's life and colorful stories about his adventures. Instead, we have a rich collection of medical works written by several ancient Greeks. These writers were real people. These doctors saw human suffering, cared for the sick and the wounded, set bones, and performed surgery. Besides tending the ill, they tried to understand the nature of sickness and health. They were mindful of responsibilities and duties of their profession. Through their words, they show the Greek achievement of founding scientific medicine and setting standards for a compassionate medical profession. The ideas of the Hippocratic writers sowed seeds of medicine that twenty-first-century doctors practice and that you find in medical books today.

WORLD OF THE HIPPOCRATICS

WHAT AN AMAZING ERA THE HIPPOCRATIC writers saw! The physicians and teachers who wrote the Hippocratic texts lived in an age of cultural blossoming. The Greek world in the fifth (499–400) and fourth (399–300) centuries B.C. saw stunning artistic, theatrical, political, philosophical, and scientific achievements. Spectacular temples, such as the Parthenon in Athens were built. Exquisite marble sculptures of gods and men were carved by Praxiteles and other artists. Plays including Aristophanes' *Lysistrata* and Euripides' *Medea*, were first performed—comedies and dramas that still touch the feelings of modern audiences. Herodotus composed his account of the war between the Greeks and Persians—the first written work of Western history.

In Athens, this era saw the establishment of the world's first citizen government—democracy. Philosophers, including Plato and Aristotle, sought truth about the nature of the world and of humankind. The achievements of the ancient Greeks laid foundations of thought that influence the world even today. The Hippocratic writers belonged to this great age and made valuable contributions to the future.

Ancient Greece was not like any country in the modern world. No national boundary surrounded a unified Greek nation. Ancient Greece was made up of dozens of individual city-states. This type of Greek community was called a *polis*. Each polis had its own government. Some polises were ruled by kings; some by groups of wealthy land-owning citizens. After Athens shaped the first democracy in the fifth century B.C., other polises adopted that form of government. In democratic polises, male citizens participated in decision making for their community. They voted in the assembly, acted as jurors in court cases, and held public offices.

A polis included its main city as well as surrounding territory. Farmland, forests, and nearby villages belonged to the polis. A polis usually had a diverse economy with some fishing and farming, manufacturing of goods, such as pottery and iron wares, and sometimes even mines and quarries for extracting silver or marble from the ground.

Often, the polis's main city was surrounded by a defensive wall. Wars were frequent in the ancient world; a sound wall could help protect the citizens within it from invading armies. Neighborhoods of homes, as well as the government and business center of the polis, were in the wall-enclosed city. Greek cities were generally built around a hill or a large rock outcrop. Temples to the gods were built on this high ground, called an acropolis. (The acropolis in Athens, site of the Parthenon, is the most famous of these city features.) The bustling center of Greek community life was called the agora. With

The Parthenon and other handsome temples were built on the Acropolis in Athens.

shops, market stalls, government offices, and temples the agora was the downtown of ancient Greek cities.

In the Hippocratics' time, Greek cities were not only located on the peninsula and islands of modern Greece. Greek polises stood in North Africa, Asia Minor, and lands that are now in France, Italy, Russia, and Syria. Although they were not united in a single state, there were strong ties between polises. They had agreements to trade with one another and to fight to defend one another in wars.

The Hippocratic writers are connected to Cos and Cnidos. Cos is an island in the Aegean Sea close to the coast of Asia Minor, now Turkey. Cnidos is located on that nearby coast. case histories in the Hippocratic texts show that some of these doctors treated many patients in Thessaly, a region in northern Greece.

Ancient Greeks identified themselves as citizens of their home polis or city—Athenians from Athens, Coans from Cos, Cnidans from Cnidos. Beyond their polis pride, Greeks had strong cultural identity as Greeks. The ancient historian Herodotus wrote that Greeks had "shared blood, shared language, shared religion, and shared custom."[1] By "shared blood," Herodotus meant that they had Greek ancestors.

Even Greeks who lived in distant colonies traced their families to their Greek homeland. The "shared language," was Greek. Non-Greek speakers were called "barbarians." Other tongues supposedly sounded like "bar-bar" to the Greeks. Regarding their "shared religion," Greeks believed in a collection of gods and goddesses who were immortal, bigger than life, and had supernatural powers.

We know nothing about the individual lives of any of the authors of the Hippocratic Collection. From knowledge of Greek culture, though, we can surmise some things about the men who wrote it. Men and women in Greek society had vastly different roles. While women were citizens, they did not have the rights of men. They did not own property or conduct business transactions of a value greater than a small amount of barley.[2] Women's lives were centered in their homes. Public life was the realm of men. It is likely that all of the physicians and teachers who wrote the Hippocratic texts were men.

From birth, Greek religion and myths would have been part of the Hippocratics' lives. At the heart of Greek mythology was a group of twelve principal deities. These twelve gods and goddesses had human forms and complex personalities. With their powers, they could interfere in human lives. Each one had his or her special sphere of influence. Zeus was the most powerful. Poseidon was god of the sea. Aphrodite was goddess of love. Beyond these major gods, Greek mythology also had minor gods, such as the Muses, the nine goddesses of individual arts and sciences. They were also immortal, but had fewer powers than the main gods. In a third tier of mythological figures were the heroes. Heroes had powers, but they were not deathless. Asclepius, the god of healing, was of this group.

Ceremonies honoring the gods filled the Greek calendar. Greeks expressed respect for their deities through rituals. They gave gifts to the gods and sacrificed animals to them. Processions were held to honor them. Sporting events, including the Olympics, and theater productions were dedicated to the gods and intended to give them pleasure. Beautiful

The ruins of Athens' ancient agora, the center of community life, are today surrounded by the modern city.

temples were constructed to give the gods dwellings on earth. Sacrifice of animals, including cattle, sheep, goats, and even chickens, was central to Greek religion. Priests followed a ritual to kill the animal on a special altar. The meat was then roasted on an open fire. In these ceremonial events, Greeks feasted on the roasted meat.

Schools for boys were well established by the Hippocratics' time. Boys typically began classroom education when they were about seven years old. As girls were expected to grow up to be wives and mothers, most did not have formal education outside of the home. In schools, boys learned to read and write. They memorized poetry—especially Homer's poems, the *Iliad* and the *Odyssey*—and learned to play a musical instrument, often the lyre. Athletics were also taught. Boys ran, practiced throwing the discus and javelin, and wrestled. As schools were private, a family's wealth influenced their sons' training. Boys who were needed to work, studied shorter times. Sons of prominent families could afford years of education. Wealthy boys were accompanied to school by a family slave.

Scientific Thought

The Greeks' rich mythology provided explanations about natural phenomena—Zeus could strike lightning bolts. Poseidon could cause earthquakes. Storms, eclipses, seasons, and other events could be viewed as acts of deities. Even before the Hippocratics, some Greeks began looking for explanations in nature. Instead of finding answers in myths, they sought rational sequences of cause and effect. They did not give up their religion; they still respected their deities, but their curiosity led them to consider more earthbound explanations.[3]

One early thinker named Thales lived from approximately 640 to 546 B.C. Thales thought that there must be one original substance that was the basis of all things. He suggested that this substance was water. Thales proposed that "the Earth is held up by water and rides like a ship and when it is said to 'quake' it is then rocking because of the movement of the water."[4] Instead of crediting Poseidon, the "earth-shaker," with these events, Thales was seeking a natural cause.

Anaximander, a contemporary of Thales, was curious about the heavens as well as substances. He proposed a model to explain the observed movements of the sun, moon, and stars. Earth

A map of the Mediterranean Sea and some Greek polises of the Hippocratics' time.

was shaped like a cylinder with the inhabited lands on the top, suggested Anaximander. The heavenly bodies were in three rings of fire revolving around this flat-topped cylinder. Anaximander also proposed a theory of the origins of animals, including man. In myths, men were made by the gods. In Anaximander's view, animals were created from the "wet." Man,

29

he suggested was originally born to a kind of fish.[5]

Other Greek thinkers proposed their views of the earth and the heavens and explanations for change. As Greek scientific thought was taking shape, it is clear that there was an open, public quality to their quests for knowledge. Thinkers knew of one another's ideas and criticized and discussed them. Theories that could not stand up to scrutiny were rejected. Those that seemed plausible were often developed in greater detail by subsequent thinkers.

Empedocles was born in about 493 B.C., about thirty years before Hippocrates was supposedly born. Empedocles suggested that there were four original and simple elements. These were fire, air, earth, and water. Although called elements, these were not the same as the 117 chemical elements recognized today. Empedocles theorized that all substances of the world were made of the four elements, mixed and remixed into different substances. The proportions of these elements determined the substances. Bone, for example, he believed was four parts fire, two parts water, and two parts earth.[6] The four elements of Empedocles' philosophy endured in Greek science and medicine for many years.

3

EARLIER MEDICINE

ATHENA, THE GODDESS OF WAR FOR righteous causes, among other things, was one of the twelve principal Greek deities. According to myths, this daughter of Zeus was born an adult. She supposedly leaped fully formed, armed for battle, from her father's head. Unlike Athena, Hippocratic medicine did not burst forth so suddenly.

The Hippocratic physicians wrote most of their works between 430 and 330 B.C. In the years before they put pen to papyrus, Greeks already had medical traditions and healers. The Hippocratic doctors raised medicine to a higher level, one with a scientific point of view and expectations of physicians' responsibilities.

Looking at Greek medicine before the Hippocratics, we can see the context of their achievement.

Homer's Healers

Among the richest sources of information about early Greeks are the great epic poems attributed to Homer. The *Iliad* and the *Odyssey* were composed between 725 and 675 B.C. The two tales were inspired by and are set in an earlier time. The *Iliad* tells about events during the Trojan War, a long and violent conflict. The *Odyssey* recounts the adventures of one of the war heroes on his long journey home. With Achilles' rage, King Priam's love of his son, Odysseus's dog's loyalty, these powerful poems are still exciting and moving. They reveal a great deal about ancient Greek beliefs, society, values, and customs. They also give us glimpses of early Greek ideas about illness and healing.

In Homer's poems, there are both supernatural and human causes for illness and injuries. Gods inflict some diseases and wounds;

they also intervene to heal them. Many wounds, though, have earthly causes. The *Iliad* takes place during a war. Greek and Trojan warriors fought with spears and arrows. Homer paints a vivid picture of battle and its bloodshed. More than a hundred different wounds are described in the poem, some with gory realism.

As the *Iliad* opens, Apollo, the archer god and patron of arts and sciences, is angry with one of the Greek kings. Enraged by Agamemnon's disrespect for one of his priests, Apollo "swept a fatal plague through the army."[1] He launched arrows of plague at the Greeks. Disease then "cut them down in droves—and the corpse fires burned on night and day, no end in sight."[2] After many warriors had perished, Agamemnon relented and did as Apollo's priest had asked. To get back into the god's favor, the Greeks then "sacrificed to Apollo full grown bulls and goats . . . and savory smoke went swirling up to the skies."[3] Satisfied with Agamemnon's actions and the abundant sacrifice, Apollo stopped the plague.

The *Iliad* also shows Apollo's healing powers. When a Trojan soldier, Glaucus, is wounded, he prays, "Hear me, Lord Apollo! Wherever you are now . . . wherever on earth, you can hear a man in pain, you have that power, and pain comes on me now. Look at this ugly wound—my whole arm rings with stabbing pangs, the blood won't clot, my shoulder's a dead weight . . . I beg you, Apollo, heal this throbbing wound, lull the pain now, lend me power in battle."[4] Apollo answered Glaucus's prayer. "He stopped the pains at once, stanched the dark blood in his throbbing wound and filled his heart with courage."[5] Glaucus was cured.

Homer shows a human side of battlefield medicine. "A man who can cut out shafts and dress our wounds—a good healer is worth a troop of other men," states a Greek general. Machaon, a doctor, had just been struck by a Trojan arrow.[6] Machaon was rushed out of battle to safety because be was so valuable to the armies. Machaon and his brother, Podalirius, appear several times in the *Iliad*. Both brothers are physicians. Their home is Thessaly, in northern Greece. Beyond being doctors, they command their own armies and brought forty ships to the war. Both fight gallantly on the battlefield.

Machaon and Podalirius are identified by Homer as sons of Asclepius. Asclepius is an important figure in Greek medicine. In the *Iliad*, Asclepius seems to be a mortal man. In later traditions, Asclepius's identity changed. Instead of being seen as a man, he became a hero with powers of a minor god.[7] In these later myths, Asclepius was the son of Apollo and the nymph Coronis. As a hero, he was credited with miraculous cures and was worshipped as a god of healing. Later, around the Greek world, and even later in the Roman Empire, special healing sanctuaries called Asclepia were dedicated to him.

In the *Iliad*, Machaon applies his medical skills. Redheaded Menelaus, King Agamemnon's brother, was hit by an arrow shot by a Trojan warrior. Blood gushed from Menelaus's wound.

This Roman marble statue of Asclepius is believed to be a copy of a Greek statue from the fifth century B.C. The hero/god is holding his staff with the snake wrapped around it.

Machaon was summoned from the fighting. First, Machaon pulled out the arrow, right through Menelaus's armor. He then removed the punctured armor. Machaon sucked out some of Menelaus's blood, cleansing the wound. Finally, he applied healing ointments.[8] With Machaon's effective first aid, Menelaus recovered. There is nothing supernatural or magical about Machaon's straightforward care of this injury.

The *Odyssey* offers another view of medical care. When he was a boy, Odysseus was out hunting wild boar with two young men. Odysseus's spear struck the boar, but the animal turned on him. The boar's sharp tusk slashed Odysseus's thigh, gouging a deep wound. His two companions skillfully bandaged Odysseus's leg. They "chanted an old spell that stanched the blood."[9] In this case, the wound was treated by mortal men who used a combination of human skill and magic.

In Homer, we see three types of successful medical treatment of injuries. The god Apollo has supernatural powers that heal Glaucus's wounds. Machaon, a mortal man, uses medical skills that set Menelaus on the road to recovery. Finally, young Odysseus's friends use first aid combined with magic spells to treat his injury.

Physicians and Koinon

Looking at the time and people that led to the Hippocratic physicians, it is important to remember that medicine in ancient Greece was not a profession in the modern sense. There were no qualifications to be a doctor; no medical schooling, examinations, or licenses were required. A variety of people dealt with different aspects of health. Midwives delivered babies, herbalists prepared remedies, trainers at gymnasia worked with athletes who competed in games at events including the Olympics. Some practitioners claimed to treat illnesses with magic charms and incantations.[10]

There were no regulations for becoming a doctor, but by the fifth century (499–400) B.C., in some parts of Greece there were medical groups. In different trades, Greeks had organizations like

This Roman mosaic floor from Cos dates from several centuries after Hippocrates' time. It shows Asclepius arriving on Cos in a boat. He is met by a fisherman and Hippocrates, who is seated and wearing white robes.

guilds, called koinon. Bronze workers and potters, for example, had their own koinon. These organizations were recognized by the polis. A koinon set its own rules for membership and had its own officials.[11]

Two medical koinon, one on Cos and one in nearby Cnidos, are known to have existed. Their members were known as Asclepiads. A decree inscribed in stone discovered at the sanctuary at Delphi recognizes their privileges there. "It has pleased the association (koinon) of the Asclepiads of Cos and Cnidos: that if the Asclepiad on arriving at Delphi desires to consult the oracle or to sacrifice, he should swear among the Delphians before consultation that he is an Asclepiad," it reads in part.[12] The sacred precinct of Delphi with its temples, treasuries, theater, and stadium was regarded as the center of the Greek world. Delphi was home to the Delphic oracle, a priestess who made prophecies inspired by Apollo. The Asclepiads were clearly important to be so recognized in Delphi. The wording of the decree implies a connection between the Coans and Cnidans. Another Asclepiad clan or koinon may have existed on the island of Rhodes at an earlier time.

These koinon were identified with Asclepius, the hero god. According to at least one ancient source, the Asclepiads of Cos and Cnidos were considered descendants of Podalirius, Asclepius's son and Machaon's brother in the *Iliad*.[13] The Asclepiads considered themselves to be blood descendants of Asclepius or otherwise connected to him as practitioners of healing arts. In the Asclepiad koinon, medical knowledge was passed down through families.[14] Fathers taught their sons, who in turn taught their sons. Instruction was probably similar to an apprenticeship; a young man assisted an established physician, learning at his side.[15]

Beyond the Asclepiads of Cos and Cnidos, there were other doctors in fifth century B.C. Greece. Scattered references mention private physicians in the service of kings and public physicians paid by polises. Herodotus, in his history written around 430 B.C., sheds some light on Greek medicine. He wrote about a famous physician named Democedes from Croton. Croton was located in what is now southern Italy. According to Herodotus, "physicians from Croton were said to be the best throughout Hellas."[16] (Hellas was the name Greeks used for Greece.) After Democedes argued with his father, he moved to the island of Aegina. In Aegina, even though he did not have instruments or equipment, "he surpassed the other physicians there." The people of Aegina hired him "at state expense." They paid him one talent. A talent was a unit of weight, often of silver, that was used as currency. Later, Democedes was hired by the Athenians for more money.[17] Then he moved on to Samos and was paid even more. This escalating service shows not only that Democedes was a rising medical star, but also that the Greeks sometimes hired public physicians.

Democedes' fortunes turned when he was on Samos. He was taken prisoner by the Persians. Darius, king of Persia, dislocated his ankle when dismounting from his horse. Darius's Egyptian physicians "employed violent remedies to treat it." Still suffering, Darius heard that the prisoner Democedes might be able to help him. Democedes was reluctant to be a traitor to Greece by treating Darius. When threatened by torture, he changed his mind. Democedes "employed Greek remedies." He first used "vigorous treatments" then "gentle ones" and "he made sure that Darius got some sleep."[18] Soon Darius was restored to health, and he rewarded Democedes generously.[19] Herodotus's stories are sometimes exaggerated and not completely reliable. The specifics of Democedes' tale may not be accurate, but the account still shows us attitudes and medical practices of that time.

4

HIPPOCRATES OF COS

ACCORDING TO TRADITION, HIPPOCRATES was born on the island of Cos in about 460 B.C. He reputedly taught at or directed a medical school there. Long lived, his death is often dated at 380 B.C. Only these scraps of biographical information about Hippocrates are widely accepted. Even these are questioned by some scholars.

Ancient Greeks admired the ideas expressed in the Hippocratic writings. These texts offered valuable practical training and non-religious theories of illness. They set high standards for patient-centered medical care. Greeks came to think of the author of these works as the ideal physician—a wise, experienced, and caring doctor.[1] Legends and colorful stories about this doctor Hippocrates were written and repeated. With the many jumbled references to Hippocrates passed down through the centuries, it is impossible to sift truth from fiction.

A biography of Hippocrates believed to be written by a physician named Soranus in the first century still exists. Soranus lived five hundred years after Hippocrates' time. (This would be similar to someone writing today about Ferdinand Magellan's explorations in the 1500s.) We do not know if the Soranus biography was based on reliable information or on repeated fiction. Possibly some tidbits, such as the names of Hippocrates' parents, Heraclides and Phenaretes, are accurate.

Galen, the next most famous ancient physician after Hippocrates, was profoundly influenced by Hippocratic medicine. Born in Pergamum in Asia Minor about A.D. 130, Galen was Greek but living at the time of the Roman Empire in a city of the Roman Empire, and he was a Roman citizen. The son of a prominent land-owning family, Galen was well educated and widely traveled. As a young man, he studied in

Hippocrates and Galen are each at times called the "Father of Medicine." In this 1677 engraving, they are pictured together. Note that where Hippocrates is touching the seedling, it has burst into bloom.

Alexandria, then he returned to Pergamum where he was surgeon to gladiators. Gladiators fought with spears, swords, and their fists in brutal athletic contests. He undoubtedly had a great deal of experience in dealing with their wounds. Galen then traveled to Rome where he was appointed physician to the emperor's son. A prolific writer, Galen is credited with composing more than five hundred texts, including many medical tracts. More than one hundred of his works still exist.[2]

Galen's idealization of Hippocrates influenced later understanding of the legendary physician. Galen believed that Hippocrates was a real historic man, a doctor, teacher, and medical writer. Although he recognized that Hippocrates was not the author of all of the Hippocratic Collection, he believed that many of the texts were Hippocrates' own. Galen wrote detailed lists identifying authentic texts. He also indicated those that he thought were written by students or followers of Hippocrates. In his sorting, Galen identified the texts that most agreed with his own ideas and that he found inspiring

as the genuine ones.[3] Galen considered
Hippocrates the founder of the medical theory
that there were four elements or humors in the
human body and that these were acted on by
four opposite qualities—hot, cold, dry, and wet.
Galen expanded this theory.

A brief look at ancient references to
Hippocrates and a quick look at Cos will not
conclude disputes about the famed doctor.
These can, however, give us a vague picture of
one possible Hippocrates.

Philosophers' Words

The Greek philosopher Plato lived from 427
until 347 B.C. Plato is admired as one of the
greatest thinkers of all times. The word
philosophy comes from two ancient Greek roots;
philo means "love of," *sophia* means "knowledge."
A philosopher is one who loves knowledge. Plato
devoted his life to seeking knowledge. Plato's
writings are still thought provoking. Most of
Plato's works are framed as dialogues between a
teacher named Socrates and students. The
dialogues are not historic accounts of real

conversations; they express Plato's philosophy. Plato's works provide glimpses of Greeks of his time—including Hippocrates.

Plato's dialogue titled *Protagoras* was written in the early fourth century B.C., but is set a few decades earlier, around 430 B.C. In it, Socrates is talking with a young man named Hippocrates. Hippocrates was a fairly common name. Socrates asks the young man:

> Suppose for instance you had it in mind to go to your namesake Hippocrates of Cos, the doctor, and pay him a fee on your own behalf, and someone asked you in what capacity you thought of Hippocrates with the intention of paying him, what would you answer?
>
> I should say in his capacity as a doctor.
>
> And what would you hope to become?
>
> A doctor.[4]

In another of Plato's dialogues, the *Phaedrus,* Socrates and a student are discussing the human soul. The soul, they suggest, should be

The Renaissance painter Raphael depicted the philosophers Plato and Aristotle together in this 1509 work titled *School of Athens*. Plato, the older philosopher, is pointing up, symbolizing his view that ideas and eternal forms are the ultimate reality. On the right, Aristotle gestures toward the ground symbolizing his search for truth in the things of the world.

considered as a whole, rather than in parts. "If we are to believe Hippocrates, the Asclepiad, we can't understand even the body without such a procedure," Phaedrus says to Socrates. Socrates responds, "No, my friend and he is right. But we must not just rely on Hippocrates; we must examine the assertion and see whether it accords with the truth."[5]   Phaedrus and Socrates then continue their inquiry into the nature of the soul.

Plato's brief references reveal several details about Hippocrates. First, they show that a physician named Hippocrates from Cos was famous enough to be known in Athens. The *Protagoras* also shows that students could pay Hippocrates to be trained as doctors. This may be a departure from earlier traditional medicine taught mostly by doctor fathers to their sons. Plato's comments also show that Hippocrates was known as an Asclepiad. This connects to accounts of the Asclepiads of Cos.

Another reference to Hippocrates is found in the writings of the philosopher, Aristotle. In his book, *Politics*, Aristotle considered factors that make a polis great. Being big, with a large population, he wrote, was not most important. Rather, a polis's superiority was in its power to accomplish its objectives. As a comparison, he noted, "as a person might say, that Hippocrates was a greater physician, though not a greater man, than one that exceeded him in the size of his body."[6] Aristotle, who lived from 384 to 322 B.C., confirms Hippocrates' fame. This quote also implies that Hippocrates was not a physically large man.

Cos

If any one thing is true about Hippocrates, it is that he was from the island of Cos. This sun-drenched island is popular with beachgoers and tourists today. The island has many Hippocrates-related attractions. A modern bronze statue of Hippocrates stands in a harborside park; a very old plane tree in a small square is known as the Hippocrates Tree. According to legend, Hippocrates taught in the shade of this tree—

Rocky Mount Dikaios forms the jagged backbone of the island of Cos. Forests, groves of olive trees, and pastures cloak its lower elevations. The island also has fertile farmland. Agriculture continues on Cos, but tourism is now a major industry there.

but the tree is perhaps five hundred years old and the physician lived 2,400 years ago.

In the Cos museum, a mosaic floor from a third century Roman house depicts Hippocrates, a fisherman, and the healing god Asclepius. Tickets for the archaeological site of the healing sanctuary, the Asclepion, are decorated with a picture of Hippocrates, even though its construction was not started until after the date usually stated for his death.

Southeast of Athens, in the Aegean Sea, Cos stands just off the coast of Asia Minor. Long and narrow, Cos stretches twenty-eight miles from end to end, but it is only seven miles wide at its broadest. Looking to the east from Cos, the Turkish coast is clear across a short stretch of sea. The peninsula of Bodrum, site of the ancient city of Halicarnassus, is only three miles from Cos. A bit further south, the peninsula of Cnidos, which was home to another ancient Greek medical center, is about ten miles across the water from the island.

A jagged spine of mountains runs through the center of the southern part of Cos. Mount Dikaios, with its rocky summit and sheer cliffs, juts 2,780 feet high. In the north part of the island is a fertile plateau; fine farmland extends from there along the coast in the shadow of the mountains. With springs and mountain streams, Cos has more fresh water than many Greek islands.

Located in a region of volcanic activity, Cos also has hot, mineral-rich springs that bubble up from the ground and in the sea. Earthquakes regularly rock the island. The ancient Greek historian Thucydides commented on one devastating earthquake in Cos in 412 B.C. The city on Cos, he wrote, "had been lately laid in ruins by an earthquake, by far the greatest in living memory, and . . . the inhabitants had fled to the mountains."[7] If Hippocrates' dates are accurate, he would have been forty-eight years old at that time. Even today, seismic activity occasionally rattles Coan hotels and cafés.

In the fifth century B.C., Cos was apparently not a major political or military force.[8] During the early years of that century, Cos was under Persian rule. The widespread Persian Empire controlled vast territory to the east of Greece. Greeks and Persians had a history of enmity.

Persia launched military campaigns against Greece in 499, 490, and 480 B.C. After the Persians were pushed back, an alliance of Greek polises, known as the Delian Confederacy, was founded in 478 B.C. Polises remained independent, but in joining the Delian Confederacy, they paid taxes for their defense and pledged to fight together. Athens was the wealthiest and most powerful of the Greek polises in the alliance. By 450 B.C., Cos was a member of the confederacy and an ally of Athens. Cos's assessment was five talents. Wealthy states paid as much as thirty talents, poor polises paid less than two talents.[9] From the tax payment, it appears that Cos was middle class; neither wealthy nor impoverished.

With groves of olive trees, fields of grain, and goats nibbling on mountainside pastures, Cos provided for her people. Coans fished and farmed. The islanders were prosperous enough to have their own local money. Their early silver coins had a picture of a crab on one side and an athlete, a discus thrower, on the reverse.[10]

The Hippocrates Tree is on Cos. According to local legend, Hippocrates taught his medical students by this aged plane tree. The tree is so old and fragile now that its branches are supported by metal scaffolding. Although the tree is not possibly old enough to have shaded the great physician, perhaps he taught in the shade of a similar tree on the island.

The most important town of fifth century B.C. on Cos was Astypalaea, which translates to "old city." The most important town of the fifth century B.C. on Cos is known as Astypalea, which translates to "old city." This city was located on the west end of the island. Small hamlets and hill communities were scattered through the countryside. Few archaeological sites from Hippocrates' time have been excavated. Around 365 B.C., a new main city was established on the east end of the island. This center flourished and is the site of modern Cos. Archaeologists have uncovered many fine Greek structures and later Roman temples, houses, baths, and a lovely amphitheater there.

Medical School of Cos

Imagining Hippocrates in Cos, if we are very cautious, we can find a slight shadow of a real historic man. It seems likely that he was a member of a medical family that in some way considered themselves descendents of Asclepius. This family was probably somewhat aristocratic.

As a boy, a young Asclepiad would likely learn to read and write, study poetry and music, and train at sports. Beyond this conventional education, he probably learned medicine from his father and grandfather. Cos, at this time already had its reputation for medicine and an established koinon, or association, of physicians.

Hippocrates' name is often connected to a medical school on Cos—sometimes he is credited as its founder or director. No one knows what this school looked like or where it was located on the island. In Athens, in about 380 B.C., the philosopher Plato founded a school known as the Academy in a parklike setting. At Plato's Academy, instruction between older thinkers and students was informal . On Cos, the medical school may have been an extension of the physicians' koinon.[11] Perhaps teachers and students met at a private house with gardens. Possibly they met in a public building with space for lectures. For now, questions about this famous school remain unanswered.

At the Cos center, medical education opened from its traditional family basis to allow nonfamily members to train to be doctors. From Plato's comments and the *Hippocratic Oath,* it is clear that young men could enroll in medical studies. They could pay fees to be trained as physicians.

The Cos medical school earned a reputation for its rational medicine. Many famous doctors of the fourth century B.C. were trained in Cos and then went on to care for patients in other places. Dracon, Thessalus, and Polybus, reportedly Hippocrates' sons and son in law, were Coan trained doctors. Alexander the Great's personal physician was a Coan physician named Critodemus. Alexander's father, Philip of Macedon, had his eye injury treated by the Coan Critobulus. History has also preserved the names of Apollonius, Dexippus, and Praxagoras, other Coan physicians.[12] Perhaps some of these famed medical men were trained by the historic Hippocrates.

5

SCIENCE OF MEDICINE

AT FIRST GLANCE, THE SCIENCE OF THE Hippocratics looks very different from the science we know today. These ancient doctors did not have stethoscopes to listen to the sounds of beating hearts or breathing lungs. They did not have X-rays to see broken bones inside the body. The Hippocratics did not even have thermometers and microscopes. Yet, they were founders of scientific medicine.

The Hippocratics, unlike earlier healers, forged this new approach to medicine by making observations and searching for natural causes. These are still cornerstones of scientific inquiry. Like modern scientists, Hippocratic physicians made systematic and meticulous observations over prolonged periods of time.[1] They examined and attentively observed patients and kept detailed records of patients' symptoms during the course of illnesses.

The Hippocratics also sought causes of illnesses. Just as Thales and others looked for natural explanations for phenomena like earthquakes, the Hippocratics looked for natural causes for ailments. These physicians believed that health was the normal state. If a person was not healthy, then there must be a cause that brought about the effect of ill health.[2] Hippocratic doctors used the tools that they had available—observations of their senses and their powers of reasoning. In their searching, they rejected the idea that supernatural forces, like the gods, sent causes or cures.

Empirical observation is essential to scientific method. Empirical is sometimes defined as pertaining to or founded upon experiment or experience. We use our senses to make empirical observations. An empirical observation, for example, is that a dropped rock falls to earth. A nonempirical observation is that the rock is beautiful. The sense of sight is widely used in observations. You can see the sun rise in the east or see a train race by or see an old tomato's brown spots. Other senses can be used in empirical observations—you can feel the heat of the sun. Hear the change in the sound of an approaching train. Smell the unpleasant odor of the rotting tomato. Even the sense of taste can be used in empirical observations—the salty taste of seawater, for example.

A single observation is not enough to be useful in a scientific inquiry. Observe the rising sun from the same place long enough, and you see the seasonal pattern of the sun rising progressively further north, then reversing and rising further to the south. If you continue your observations you will see this pattern repeated year after year. Sit by the railroad tracks and hear dozens of trains; the pitch of the whistle of every train is higher as it approaches you, then it is suddenly lower as it passes. Set several tomatoes on the windowsill. After a few days, you will notice that each one has a nasty smell, evidence of chemical changes in the fruit.

The Hippocratic Collection provides many examples of physicians making systematic empirical observations. The physicians used all five of their senses—sight, smell, touch, sound, and even taste.[3] Some Hippocratic texts list specific signs a physician should observe. Other volumes are records of observations of patients.

First study the patient's *facies* [face]; whether it has a healthy look and in particular whether it be exactly as it normally is. If the patient's normal appearance is preserved, this is best; just as the more abnormal it is, the worse it is. The latter appearance may be described thus: the nose sharp, the eyes sunken, the temples fallen in, the ears cold and drawn in and their lobes distorted, the skin of the face hard, stretched and dry, and the colour of the face pale or dusky.[4]

The doctor notes the signs he sees—the patient's appearance. He also records signs that he feels—the patient's cold ears and dry skin. Hippocratic doctors used their hearing to listen to breathing and coughs. They noted the smell of the patients' stool. They even tasted blood, urine, mucus, and tears.[5] While some of these tests sound unpleasant and even unhealthy to us, at the same time we recognize these doctors' thoroughness in using the tools they had available—their own senses.

Case studies documented in the volume titled *Epidemics* give us a picture of these physicians' systematic observations of patients. Forty-two straightforward case histories are listed. These patients were men and women who lived and fell ill 2,500 years ago. Some recovered, others did not. Each case study begins with a brief introduction of the patient and his or her initial state. Concise daily observations are recoded, as well as the patient's final outcome.

> The lad who lay by the Liars' Market took a fever as the result of exhaustion. . . .

> First Day: bowels disordered with copious thin bilious stools; urine thin, rather dark; insomnia, thirst.

Second day: all symptoms more pronounced. . . . No sleep; his mind was disordered; slight sweating.

Third day: uneasy, thirst, nausea, much tossing about, distress, delirium, extremities cold and livid...

Fourth day: no sleep; condition deteriorated.

Seventh day: died.

Age about twenty.[6]

Some patients' descriptions are very lengthy. A man "with heaviness of the head," had his symptoms described for many of the forty days he was ill before recovering. Cleanactides, who lived near the temple of Heracles, was sick for eighty days before his health was restored.[7]

Hippocratic doctors considered health to be the body's natural condition. If one was not healthy, there must be a cause for the illness or condition. External causes of wounds and injuries were often easy to explain—a sword wound in a warrior's leg, bones in a child's arm

The title page of the Greek edition of the Hippocratic collection published in Venice in 1526.

broken in a fall. Causes of diseases, internal conditions, even infections, were far more elusive. The Greeks knew nothing of bacteria or viruses. Germ theory would not be discovered for another 2,300 years. Causes of some diseases are mysteries even today. Even though the Hippocratics had no chance of discovering most causes, they were resolute in looking for explanations in nature. Internal imbalances and environmental influences, such as climate and water, were among the causes they proposed.

The Hippocratics' position that health was governed by nature, not the gods, is clearly laid out in the text titled *The Sacred Disease*. This text addresses epilepsy, a disorder of the nervous system. People with epilepsy sometimes suffer seizures. A seizure is caused by a surge of electrical activity in the brain. The surge may cause uncontrolled movements.

Epilepsy was called the sacred disease because some Greeks believed that seizures were sent by the gods. The author of *The Sacred Disease* completely rejected that idea. "I do not believe that the 'sacred disease' is any more divine or sacred than any other disease, but on the contrary, has specific characteristics and a definite cause," he wrote.[8]

The writer derided those who claimed to treat it with "purification and incantation," such as potions and charms. He asserted that those who considered it sacred were "the sort of people we now call witch-doctors, faith-healers, quacks and charlatans."[9] He denounced their superstitious treatments. Their treatments included prohibitions on wearing black, sleeping on goatskin, or putting one foot or hand upon another. *The Sacred Disease* asserted that epilepsy is hereditary, which is now known to be true in some, but not all, cases. This author also correctly suggested that seizures originate in the brain.

The writer of *The Sacred Disease* was perceptive about the brain. It is, he said, "the source of our pleasure, merriment, laughter and amusement, as of our grief, pain, anxiety and tears." He continued, "It is specially the organ which enables us to think, see and hear, and to distinguish the ugly and the beautiful, the bad and the good, pleasant and unpleasant."[10]

The author of *The Sacred Disease* rejected supernatural causes for epilepsy. He did not, however, reject religion. The gods are pure, he wrote, and they do not pollute the bodies of mankind.[11]

The authors of *The Sacred Disease* and of *The Heart* showed some understanding of human organs. In other texts, we see Greek doctors' familiarity with the human skeleton—bones and joints. Overall, though, these physicians had very little knowledge of anatomy. Anatomy is the science of the bodily structure of living things—in this case, human beings. Dissection is the process of disassembling something (such as body) to study its internal structure. Greeks did not believe in interfering with dead human bodies. Dissection was simply not practiced at their time. These doctors had never seen a human heart, lungs, or any other internal organs.[12]

From seeing the butchering of goats, cattle, and other animals, doctors may have shaped some ideas about systems of mammals. In the Hippocratic collection, it is clear that these physicians did not have much knowledge of respiratory, neurological, reproductive, digestive, or circulatory systems.

Not long after the Hippocratics, in about 345 B.C., the philosopher Aristotle began dissecting animals to understand their anatomy.[13] In the next century, dissection was practiced by Greek physicians in Alexandria, Egypt. Finally, doctors saw inside human bodies. The Alexandrian physicians made great strides in understanding organs, such as the heart, the lungs, and the liver.

Humors

The Hippocratic Collection was written by different authors over a period of decades. These writers likely lived in different places. Most seem to have been doctors, but some were probably professional teachers. All of the Hippocratic writings deal with aspects of health and medicine. Different views and sometimes conflicting views are expressed in them. Certain themes are evident in multiple texts. One recurring theme is the idea of balance and imbalance in the body.

The Four Humors

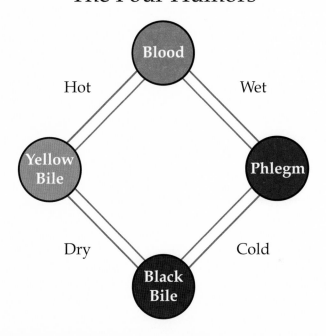

Hippocratics considered some conditions to be caused by imbalance of bodily fluids. One Hippocratic text in particular, *The Nature of Man*, discussed the four humors and qualities associated with them. The theory of humors became one of the dominant theories of ancient medicine and survived for centuries.

A system of medicine known as humorialism appears in varied forms in the collection. This theory, the theory of humors, dominated Western medicine into the 1800s.[14]

According to the theory of humors, illness is the result of disturbance to the natural balance of substances in the body or one of its parts.[15] Diet, lifestyle, and environment can all influence this balance. Different Hippocratics had different views of the substances that were supposed to be in balance.

The root of the word *humor* in Greek means "fluid or juice." The human body, we now know to be about 65 percent water. Blood, sweat, saliva, and tears, are among our bodies' fluids. Some are evident when we are ill, such as mucus when we have a head cold and diarrhea when we have digestive problems.

In the Hippocratic writings, imbalances of two body fluids, phlegm and bile, are frequently considered causes of disease.[16] Phlegm is mucus and other material produced by the lining of the respiratory tract, sometimes also called sputum.

Bile is a digestive juice produced by the liver. Two of the Hippocratic texts, *On Diseases* and *On the Nature of Man*, refer to four humors. Bile is divided into two types, black and yellow, and blood is added to the list.[17] The theory of four humors resembles the Greeks' theory of four primary elements, suggested by the philosopher Empedocles and others. (Those elements were earth, water, fire, and air.)

On the Nature of Man develops this theory of humors further. The author attributes pairs of qualities to each of the humors. These qualities are hot, cold, wet, and dry. Blood, for example, was seen to have the qualities hot and wet, like fire and water.[18] The qualities were also linked to the seasons. Cold and wet phlegm was associated with cold, wet winter, when people are prone to colds. Blood was identified with wet, hot Greek springtime.[19] According to the philosopher Aristotle, *On the Nature of Man* was written by Polybus, believed to be Hippocrates' son-in-law.

The theory of humors had a practical side. Hippocratic doctors had very few tools for treating disease. In trying to restore the proper balance of fluids, many treatments dealt with diet, baths, and rest. These therapies often allowed a body to heal itself.

While the theory of humors was vague in most Hippocratic writings, in later times it became more precise. Galen, the most influential ancient medical writer after Hippocrates, wrote extensively about the four humors. He linked them to the four elements and qualities. Within these, he suggested that there were natural mixtures and temperaments. The theory of humors was later extended to even relate to points in the heavens and constellations.[20]

6

THE ART OF MEDICINE

"LIFE IS SHORT, AND THE ART LONG; THE occasion fleeting; experience fallacious, and judgment difficult."[1] Those are the opening words of one of the most widely read works in the Hippocratic Corpus. It is titled *Aphorisms*. An aphorism is a short statement of a principle or general truth. The "art" in this aphorism is the art of medicine.

The honesty of this aphorism still resonates. Doctors today still deal with life and death. At times, they see patients' lives cut short by disease or injury. Physicians also see that their own lives are short—every doctor's knowledge is built on the discoveries and achievements of doctors and medical researchers before them.[2]

Occasion is still fleeting—a patient's recovery from a stroke, heart attack, or trauma is often improved by prompt treatment. Personal experience is not always reliable—a physician must draw on more than just his or her own observations and firsthand experience. Medicine is a human endeavor. In the end, today as in ancient Greece, doctors use their judgment to treat their patients. Practicing medicine is still an art.

The Hippocratic physicians worked to understand illness and health in terms of nature. They tried to find causes in the natural world, not blaming magical or supernatural forces. Even as they tried to understand disease, they had few treatments that could really bring about change in patients' conditions. For broken bones and dislocated joints, though, they had several effective tools and techniques.

Patients with a vast range of health problems went to Hippocratic doctors. Diseases such as malaria and pneumonia affected many. People suffered from eye disease, infections, ulcers, sore

These ancient medical tools discovered by archaeologists are displayed in the National Archaeological Museum in Athens, Greece. Scalpels, forceps, a splint, tools for drilling and moving bones, and tools for bleeding patients are in the collection.

throats, headaches, cancer, food poisoning, epilepsy, and more. Some patients had mental illnesses. For treatments, Hippocratic doctors relied largely on diet. They cooked and blended grains, wine, water, honey, vinegar, and herbs to make different medications.

"To help, or at least to do no harm,"[3] was the sensible and compassionate approach the Hippocratic physicians took to their patients' care. Rather than leaping into surgeries or violent treatments, their medicine focused on letting the body heal itself. Giving patients plenty of mild fluids and keeping them comfortable and resting often allowed nature do her work.

In the Hippocratic texts, we find the advice and experience of these physicians who practiced so long ago. Quick glimpses of four texts, *Prognosis, Regimen in Acute Diseases,* and the pair *On Fractures* and *On Joints,* show Hippocratic doctors applying the art of medicine.

Prognosis

Prognostication is the practice of making reasonably accurate predictions about the course of disease. This was an important approach in much Hippocratic medicine. Through prognosis, a physician recognizes the past, present, and likely future of a patient's condition:

> It seems to be highly desirable that a physician should pay much attention to prognosis. If he is able to tell his patients when he visits them not only about their past and present symptoms, but also to tell them what is going to happen, as well as to fill in details they have omitted, he will increase his reputation as a medical practitioner. . . . Moreover, he will be the better able to effect a cure if he can foretell, from the present symptoms, the future course of the disease. [However] it is impossible to cure all patients.[4]

Hippocratic doctors were attentive to signs of illnesses. *Prognosis* lays out guidelines for examining patients. Beyond looking at the patient, the doctor needs to question him or her. "The patient should be asked whether he has suffered from insomnia, from severe diarrhea, or if he has ravening hunger."[5] The doctor should especially observe the eyes. Movement of hands, shallow or distressed breathing, swelling, and fever are all among the symptoms to be observed.

Prognosis suggests the likely outcome for patients with certain sets of symptoms. Exhaling cold air indicates "death is close at hand."[6] "The quickest death is denoted by the vomiting of livid matter if it has a foul smell."[7] "The mildest fevers, and those which give the surest indications of recovery, cease on or before the fourth day."[8] Dozens of sets of signs and likely outcomes are described in this handbook-style volume.

"Anyone who is to make a correct forecast of a patient's recovery or death, or of the length of his illness, must be thoroughly acquainted with the signs and form his judgment by estimating their influence one on another, as has been described," concludes this Hippocratic writer. "The truth of those described in this treatise has been proved in Libya, in Delos, and in Scythia," he states.[9] This geographic note shows us that Hippocratic physicians were treating patients and making their careful observations in many parts of the Greek world.

GALENI IN LIBRVM HIPPOCRATIS

This 1550 woodcut from a book of Galen's medicine illustrates the artist's impression of an ancient clinic. Physicians are portrayed treating a variety of patients.

Regimen

Doctors today, like their Hippocratic counterparts, emphasize the importance of a healthy regimen. Regimen in a medical context is diet, exercise, and therapy to maintain or improve health. Today, recommendations for good regimen include a diet rich in fresh fruits and vegetables and low in fats and sugars. Regular aerobic and strength building exercises are advised. For people recovering from injuries, regimen may include ice packs for swelling, warm water for sprains, and physical therapy exercises.

In *Regimen in Acute Diseases*, the physician laid out treatment for pneumonia, pleurisy, and two other diseases that are believed to be malaria. Pneumonia is an inflammation or infection of the lungs. Pleurisy is an inflammation of tissues around the lungs. Malaria is an infectious disease caused by parasites and transmitted by mosquitoes. Causing high fevers and shaking chills, malaria can attack internal organs. This author states:

> I assert that this study of regimen is much to be recommended, and it is something closely allied to the most numerous and the most vital studies which compose the science of medicine. To the sick it is a powerful aid to recovery, to the healthy a means of preserving health, to athletes a means of reaching their best form, and, in short, the means by which every man may realize his desire.[10]

Several treatments are described in *Regimen*. "Barley-gruel seems to have been correctly selected as the most suitable cereal to give in these acute diseases and I have a high opinion of those who selected it," the author wrote.[11] Barley gruel was a boiled mixture of barley and water. Easy to swallow, the thin gruel was thirst quenching and easily digested. A cereal grain rich in protein, vitamins, and minerals, barley is high in fiber. Barley gruel continues to serve as a home remedy for digestive problems.

Guidelines for giving wine, hydromel, water, and oxymel, were offered in this text. Wine was a staple of the Greek diet, often diluted with water. Hydromel is a mixture of honey and water. Oxymel is mixed vinegar and honey. Oxymel is still widely used as a folk medicine. The writer of *Regimen*, especially recommends oxymel for softening the lungs and clearing the windpipe. Medicines made from skins of grapes, saffron, pomegranates, myrtle, and herbs were prescribed for some conditions. Baths were also recommended, especially for patients with pneumonia.

In some cases, if other treatments were unsuccessful, the author of *Regimen for Acute Diseases* advised using a procedure called "bleeding." In ancient Greece and into the nineteenth century, it was thought that bleeding a patient had positive benefits. George Washington, the first president of the United States, was bled for his illnesses. In 1799, Washington developed a severe sore throat. His doctors bled him repeatedly. Many historians now believe that this treatment made him sicker and contributed to his death a few days later.

The ancient Greek technique of bleeding involved making a small cut in a vein and allowing blood to drip or pour into a bowl. The Greek idea behind bleeding was that ailments were caused by imbalances in the body's humors, or fluids. Bleeding was intended to help the body to get rid of excess blood and restore proper equilibrium. Healthy people can have some blood withdrawn with no adverse affects, but modern medicine sees no benefit to the old practice of bleeding.

Fractures and Dislocations

Two texts, *On Fractures* and *On Joints,* deal with bones and the soft tissues around them. Broken legs, bruised heels, dislocated shoulders, and amputations are among the many subjects addressed. These works lay out specific instructions for surgical procedures.

The writer of *On Fractures* stated that he had seen many blunders in setting and bandaging broken arms. Therefore, he decided to describe those mistakes and "unteach" them. He explained that when setting bones in the arm, the arm should be in a natural position that can be supported by a sling, with the hand slightly higher than the elbow. He cautioned physicians to be sensitive to the patient's pain. The bandage should be firmly applied but not squeezing the arm. Bandages should be changed regularly.[12] Doctors, he stressed, should be alert to inflammation, marked by swelling, redness, heat, and pain. For broken legs and multiple fractures, he explained how to make a splint to support the bone. There is much sound advice in this volume.

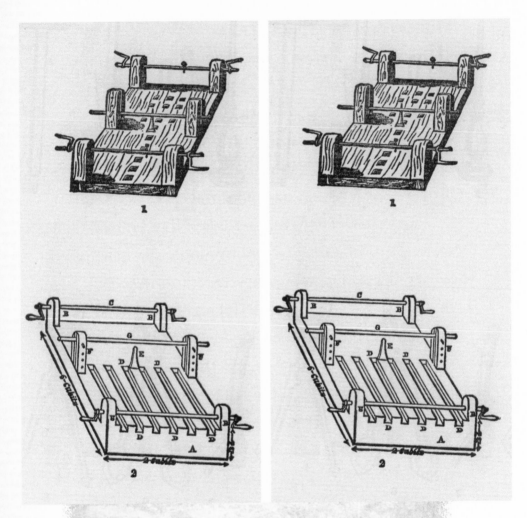

Directions for building and using a special table for treating fractures and certain dislocations were included in the text *On Joints*. Using ropes attached to the table, the physician could pull bones to separate overlapped fractures and move broken bones back into proper alignment. This device is known as a Hippocratic bench. The first image shows design of the bench. The second image shows the bench in use.

On Joints lists detailed procedures for dealing with dislocations. A dislocation occurs when a bone comes out of its proper position in a joint. Shoulders, knees, thumbs, fingers, toes, and jaws are common dislocations. In one procedure for a dislocated shoulder, the author explained, the patient should lie on the ground on his back. The physician should put a leather ball in his armpit. Another person takes hold of the patient's healthy shoulder, "so that the body may not be dragged along when the arm of the affected side is pulled."[13] A wide strap was wrapped around the ball. The physician, seated on the ground above the patient's head, held onto the strap. When everything was set, the physician pushed his foot firmly against the dislocated bone which should slip back into place. This was likely a successful procedure for many patients.

Frequent shoulder dislocations can be a serious problem. In some cases, the Hippocratic doctor would cauterize the joint to prevent further dislocations. To cauterize means to burn tissue. After the burn, scar tissue would build up at the wound, possibly reinforcing the joint. Specific instructions on using a burning hot metal poker to cauterize the shoulder are given. In that age with no painkillers, it must have been an excruciating procedure.

On Joints also told how to build and use a Hippocratic Bench. This wooden, bedlike device was useful for dislocations and for aligning broken bones. The bench had several pegs and crossbars that worked as levers and pulleys. These gave the doctor a mechanical advantage so that he could pull and manipulate bones more easily.

With these many possible treatments, the writer reminds the reader that "[t]he prime object of the physician in the whole art of medicine should be to cure that which is diseased; and if this can be accomplished in various ways, the least troublesome should be selected."[14]

THE OATH

AFTER COMPLETING FOUR YEARS OF college and earning excellent grades, physicians-in training spend four years in medical school. Two of these years are spent in classrooms and laboratories, and the last two years are spent in hospitals and clinics. Before beginning more years of training as resident physicians, the students are awarded their medical degrees at an graduation ceremony. As they stand in their caps and gowns, holding their new diplomas, they have earned the right to be called doctor and put the letters M.D. (medical doctor) after their names. At most United States medical schools, the graduates pledge an oath that has its origins in the *Hippocratic Oath*.

The *Hippocratic Oath* is the most famous of all Hippocratic works—even though most people familiar with its name have never read it. This short pledge is remarkable because, with other Hippocratic works, it laid the foundation for medical ethics. Medical ethics are the principles and values of medical conduct. Medical ethics are often in the news today as doctors and researchers face issues, such as physician-assisted suicide and whether cloning can help find cures for diseases. The *Hippocratic Oath* set standards for medical behavior.[1]

We do not know the date or author of the *Hippocratic Oath*. It is believed to have been written sometime before the first century A.D.[2] There is no indication that it was widely pledged in its early years.

Four distinct parts make up the *Hippocratic Oath*. The preamble opens the *Oath*. The covenant states the swearer's duties to his teachers and the medical community. The code states his duties to patients. Finally, the peroration affirms the oath taker's commitment to follow the terms of the *oath* into the future.[3]

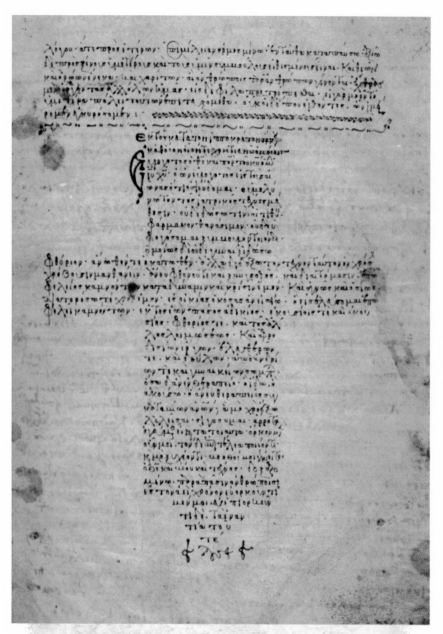

In this 12th century Byzantine manuscript, the *Hippocratic Oath* is written in the shape of a cross.

Unlike all other texts in the Hippocratic collection, the *Oath* begins with religion. The pledging doctor asks the Greek gods to be his witnesses. He swears the *Oath* to Apollo and Asclepius. Today, people still swear oaths and ask that they be witnessed by the gods of their religions. Governors, presidents, and other elected officials swear oaths of office. They often place a hand on a religious book, sometimes a Bible or a Koran, as they promise to perform the duties of their position.

The second part of the *Oath* is the covenant. In it, the oath taker states his obligations to his teacher, his teacher's family, and the medical community. He promises to act as son and brother to his teacher and his teacher's children. He also promises to share his medical knowledge with them and with others who take this oath. This oath seems to be a lifetime commitment.[4] This covenant shows that the medical profession at this time was not limited to members of medical families or clans.

The code, the third part of the *Oath,* lays out physicians' responsibilities to patients. Expected behavior and specific prohibitions on treatments are clearly stated. The principles of conduct still stand today. We expect doctors to use ability and judgment to work for the benefit of patients. We expect them to keep our confidences and not tell our secrets.

Three prohibitions in the *Oath* have been controversial. Two of these are inconsistent with other Hippocratic texts. The *Oath* states that the swearer "will not cut," which appears to mean that it does not allow surgery. Several books of the Hippocratic Corpus explain surgical techniques. Hippocratic doctors used knives to incise ulcers and infections, to cut the skull in some procedures, and to relieve fluid around the lungs. The *Oath* prohibits physicians from giving women means for abortions. Yet, one Hippocratic text on women's health explains the procedure for abortions. Its third injunction is against giving fatal drafts, or deadly medicines, to patients to end their lives. Ancient Greeks who found their pain intolerable were known to commit suicide.[5] Doctors in the ancient world were probably asked at times by patients to prescribe medicines for assisted suicide. That the *Oath* contradicts other works in the collection is interesting, but not problematic. Since these texts were written by different writers, different views would naturally be expressed.

The final statement in the *Oath* confirms that the swearer recognizes that there will be consequences if he breaks his promise. There was no law to enforce this *Oath*. The doctor who promises it expects to find a happy life, a successful practice, and even fame if he keeps his word. If he swears falsely, he expects the opposite to come his way—unhappiness and a poor reputation.

We do not know who pledged the *Hippocratic Oath* in its earliest times. It was mentioned in inscriptions on tombstones of some ancient Greek doctors.[6] In the fourth century A.D., it was being sworn by at least some doctors. The *Oath* became a respected statement of what was expected of medical professionals. As centuries passed, the *Oath* was adopted in the Christian and Islamic worlds. It was translated into

In this artist's impression of Hippocrates, the physician is writing in a book. At the time of the Hippocratics, books as we know them were not in use. These ancient doctors would have written on and read texts on sheets of papyrus that were rolled for storage.

Hebrew in the 1200s. Medical students at the University of Wittenberg in Germany pledged it in 1508. In the1800s, medical schools in Europe and North America began including it in their graduation programs.[7]

In the early twentieth century, the *Hippocratic Oath* was pledged in about one-fifth of American medical schools.[8] After World War II, people around the globe learned of atrocities committed in concentration camps in Europe. These included horrific medical experiments conducted by Nazi German physicians. Also, as the century saw amazing medical breakthroughs, questions arose about moral issues relating to medicine. Increasingly, medical schools turned to the *Hippocratic Oath* for guidance. Today, students at almost every medical school in the country pledge an oath at commencement.[9]

With the desire to pledge a meaningful promise of ethical conduct, many students and faculty found that the words of the *Hippocratic Oath* did not meet their needs. Beyond the oddity of swearing an oath to Apollo and other Greek gods, many physicians disagreed with its prohibitions. They felt that other values should be stated.

Today, there are many different oaths in the Hippocratic tradition. There are a few standard ones used by many schools. Some medical schools have their own versions. Although the words may vary, these pledges recognize the physician's responsibility to patients and have standards of conduct that define honorable behavior for physicians. At some schools, both the traditional *Hippocratic Oath* and the new oath are published in the commencement program. The *Hippocratic Oath,* as translated by J. Chadwick and W. N. Mann, is as follows:

> I swear by Apollo the healer, by Aesclepius, by Health and all the powers of healing, and call to witness all the gods and goddesses that I may keep this Oath and Promise to the best of my ability and judgement.
>
> I will pay the same respect to my master in the Science as to my parents and share my life with him and pay all my debts to him. I will regard his sons as my brothers and teach them the Science, if they desire to learn it, without fee or contract. I will hand on precepts, lectures and all other learning to my sons, to those of my master and to those pupils duly apprenticed and sworn, and to none other.
>
> I will use my power to help the sick to the best of my ability and judgement; I will abstain from harming or wronging any man by it.
>
> I will not give a fatal draught to anyone if I am asked, nor will I suggest any such thing.

Neither will I give a woman means to procure an abortion.

I will be chaste and religious in my life and in my practice.

I will not cut, even for the stone, but I will leave such procedures to the practitioners of that craft.

Whenever I go into a house, I will go to help the sick and never with the intention of doing harm or injury. I will not abuse my position to indulge in sexual contacts with the bodies of women or of men, whether they be freemen or slaves.

Whatever I see or hear, professionally or privately, which ought not to be divulged, I will keep secret and tell no one.

If, therefore, I observe this Oath and do not violate it, may I prosper both in my life and in my profession, earning good repute among all men for all time. If I transgress and forswear this Oath, may my lot be otherwise.[10]

The Ideal Physician

WITH ITS MANY VOICES, THE HIPPOCRATIC Collection documented the beginnings of rational medicine. Theories and therapies expressed in it would carry forward for centuries. Hippocratic medicine, which began emerging in about 430 B.C., was not the only medicine of the ancient Greek world. It would have lasting influence, but the history of Western medicine was not built with straight and even steps of progress.

Asclepia

At about the same time that the first Hippocratic texts were being written, the popularity of another medical practice was growing in Greece. This was religious healing, distinct from the secular or nonreligious healing of the

Hippocratics. Suddenly, there was a building boom of sanctuaries dedicated to Asclepius, the god of healing. Called Asclepia, these sanctuaries had handsome temples and altars for sacrifices. Some had sacred groves of trees. Athens, Epidaurus, Cos, Pergamum, and dozens of other Greek cities built Asclepia.

An inscribed tablet found on Cos indicates that a healing cult was established there in the late fifth or early fourth century B.C.[1] Later, between 300 and 250 B.C., construction started on an Asclepion sanctuary there.[2] With four major construction phases, the complex was expanded and embellished over a period of almost six hundred years. The sanctuary had three broad terraces sculpted into a hillside looking out to the sea. With temples, a monumental altar for sacrifices, a sacred grove of cypress trees, archways, fountains, and grand staircases, it was magnificent.

Certain procedures were followed at Asclepia. On arrival, a patient was cleansed or purified by bathing in a sacred spring. He or she would make an offering to Asclepius—an animal

Temples of the impressive Asclepion on Cos. Construction of this healing sanctuary started between 300 and 250 B.C.

sacrifice or a gift. The patient would dress in white robes and purify a second time before entering the sanctuary. Besides the priests, only patients were allowed in the sacred precinct. The patient would typically sleep one night there—in the temple, on a porch, or in special rooms. While sleeping, the patient hoped to receive a vision from Asclepius. The god himself or one of his sacred snakes or dogs might appear in the dream. Some patients were cured when they awoke the next morning.[3] Faith, rest, and a positive attitude could be a successful combination.

We know little about the relationship between the Asclepion healers and the Asclepiads and other physicians of Cos. Even though their practices were different, they may have complemented one another. Among the Asclepia, the Hippocratic physicians, and other medical practitioners, Greeks had several options for health care.

Centuries have passed since white-robed patients rested in Asclepia hopeful of divine cures. Yet, the symbol of Asclepius survives in modern medical imagery. In Greek and Roman art, the healing god was typically depicted holding a stout stick with a snake gliding around it. According to one Greek myth, Asclepius once killed a snake. As he watched, another snake, with an herb in its mouth, slithered up to the dead body. It put the herb in the lifeless creature's mouth, restoring it to life. Asclepius supposedly took the herb and revived a dead man.[4] Myths in other cultures also associate snakes with healing. The god's staff with encircling snake is called the Rod of Asclepius. Today, we see it on ambulances and badges at the center of the blue Star of Life, the emblem of Emergency Medical Services.

Alexandria

Cos was famous for its doctors. Hippocrates shines as the island's medical star, but other Coan doctors are remembered in Greek history. In the fourth century (399–300) B.C., the medical school of Cos was widely known and respected. Cos supplied doctors to many Greek rulers and states.[5] As the Cos school flourished, another great medical center was rising.

The Greek city of Alexandria, at the mouth of the Nile River in Egypt, was founded by Alexander the Great in 332 B.C. Alexander did not live to see its glory. He died in 323 B.C. and his empire was divided. Ptolemy I, a general under Alexander, won the prize of Egypt. Ptolemy and his son Ptolemy II set out to make Alexandria the cultural and intellectual center of the world. Besides building a spectacular city, this father and son also founded Alexandria's

Built on a hillside, the Co an Asclepion had three broad terraces. Used for centuries, it saw four major building phases. Temples, altars for sacrifices, broad staircases, massive retaining walls with arched niches, statues, and even fountains adorned the site.

unparalleled Museum and library. The Museum was a temple and study complex dedicated to the Muses, goddesses of the arts. Alexandria's Museum was similar to a university, attracting poets, mathematicians, astronomers, and others as students and researchers. The Ptolemies also established their library, where they strived to have all the important Greek literary works. Cos had close ties to Alexandria. Ptolemy I lived briefly on Cos; Ptolemy II was born on the island.

Many Coan doctors went to Alexandria. The medical school there was established in the early third century B.C. The Hippocratic Collection may have originally been a private collection of a doctor on Cos—perhaps someone associated with the medical school.[6] He may have taken or sent the texts to Alexandria.

Hippocratic ideas were studied in Alexandria. Alexandrian physicians also brought new knowledge to medicine. Egypt, unlike Greece at that time, allowed examination of dead human bodies. In Alexandria, doctors performed dissections. Through these studies, they saw inside the human body and recognized that blood was pumped by the heart.

Galen

Galen, who lived between A.D. 130 and 200, is the second-most famous doctor of antiquity, following only Hippocrates. In Galen's considerable body of writing, it is clear that he thought of Hippocrates as a great man, doctor, and teacher. He believed that the best ideas in the Hippocratic Collection had originated with this one extraordinary physician. Galen saw himself bringing Hippocrates' work to perfection.[7]

The blue Star of Life is the symbol of Emergency Medical Services. The staff of Asclepius is at its center. This star is often seen on ambulances and the badges of emergency medical technicians.

Many ideas from the Hippocratic Collection were carried into Galen's work. Some Hippocratic writings discussed balance of essential fluids, called humors, in the human body. Galen further refined and developed this theory. He confidently stated his theories about the humors and the forces that affected them. He prescribed treatments to reestablish their proper equilibrium. Galen also wrote extensively about anatomy. He frequently performed dissections on animals—sometimes as public demonstrations. Through dissections and his astute observations, he made substantial discoveries about the heart, the bones, the nerves, the muscles, and other body organs and tissues.[8] A philosopher as well as a doctor, Galen had strong views on the correct way to practice medicine. The physician, he believed, should have deep understanding of the human body as well as broad knowledge of therapies. The medical approach of Galen, with its Hippocratic roots, was the dominant medicine of late antiquity. Strands of it continued through medical practice of the Middle Ages.[9]

Galenic and Hippocratic medicine spread beyond the Roman Empire and medieval Europe. In the ninth century, a center of learning called the House of Wisdom was founded in Baghdad, now capital of Iraq. Many Greek scientific works were translated into Arabic there. Islamic scholars studied medical texts by both Hippocrates and Galen. Al Kindi, a multitalented thinker, wrote more than twenty medical works, including one on Hippocratic medicine.[10] Many ancient Greek works were preserved through history because of these Arabic translations.

Renaissance

In the fifteenth and sixteenth centuries, classical Greek and Roman ideas were rediscovered in Europe. This era is known as the Renaissance, which means rebirth. During the Renaissance, the invention of the moveable type printing press in 1439 for the first time made it possible to mass-produce books. With multiple copies of printed books, texts were available to more people than ever before. In 1526, a publisher in Venice published the complete works of Hippocrates.[11] The brilliance and wisdom in Hippocratic texts were available to new generations of doctors and other readers.

The rediscovery of Hippocratic medicine was accompanied by some of the same conditions that had marked its early achievement. At first, the ancient knowledge was prized as a return to fundamentals that had been lost during the Middle Ages. As doctors read and studied the texts, they were also learning from their own experiences and observations. With the new availability of books, they could read in detail about Hippocratic and Galenic theories and practices, and they could debate them with other doctors. Gradually, new theories replaced some of the ancient ones. Through the following centuries, generations of scientists made discoveries in chemistry, physiology, biology, and more. Causes of diseases were discovered. Science and technology opened new worlds of understanding.

Today, as doctors have sophisticated equipment to assist them in the examination and treatment of patients, modern medicine looks very different from that of the Hippocratics with their barley gruel and Hippocratic Benches. Looking deeper, though, we can see that principles forged by the Hippocratics are still at work. Physicians and medical researchers still look for causes and effects to explain disease. Like their ancient counterparts, today's doctors keep detailed patient case histories. With constantly updated information from medical studies, they still debate and discuss theories of health care and development of therapies. Today, more than two millennia after the *Hippocratic Oath* was written, physicians still honor responsibilities to patients, society, and their profession.

The authors of the Hippocratic texts, including Hippocrates if he did indeed write any of them, set a course for medicine that still serves us today. We still expect our doctors to be like the idealized Hippocrates—caring, wise, observant, skilled, honest, and dedicated.

ACTIVITIES

Activity 1

"Life is short, and the art long," are the opening words to the Hippocratic book titled *Aphorisms*. The art of medicine has a long history that includes the achievements of the Hippocratics. Medicine today is built on the work and discoveries of generations of doctors and researchers. Medical research occurring today is laying the groundwork for the breakthroughs of tomorrow.

By taking just a few minutes a day, you can begin to appreciate remarkable ongoing progress in medical knowledge.

Materials needed:

◈ Internet access on a computer or daily newspapers

Procedure:

Take a few minutes on each of five days to look at an online news Web site or newspaper. On the Web site, the news service may have a heading dedicated to health news. In the newspaper, you may have to look through several pages.

As you read these news sources, make a list of health-related articles. Some of the articles you find may report on studies and medical discoveries related to diseases or health conditions. Some may deal with the art of medicine, for instance, the way patients are treated in emergency rooms. Some may discuss the business of medicine, or the cost of health care.

When you have a list of several days' articles, divide your list into categories. Galen made his lists of the Hippocratic texts that he believed were authentic. In your lists, consider which of the articles address issues that would have been familiar to the Hippocratic physicians.

Activity 2

Doctors graduating from most medical schools in the United States take an oath related to the *Hippocratic Oath*. The next time you have a doctor's appointment, ask your doctor about his or her experience taking the *oath*. For some doctors, it is a very memorable experience with great symbolic meaning. Your doctor may recall whether he or she pledged the original Hippocratic Oath or an updated version.

Activity 3

Hippocratic doctors dealt with injuries as well as diseases. They bandaged cuts, set broken bones, and realigned dislocated joints. In Homer's epic poem the *Iliad* about the Trojan War, Greek doctors tended wounds on the battlefield.

While we are not likely to be struck by Trojan arrows as Homer's Greeks were, we all have occasional injuries that need care. These are usually minor cuts, splinters, burns, or sprains. Having some knowledge of first aid and proper supplies can reduce suffering and speed recovery. Families usually have first-aid kits or a collection of basic supplies.

The American Red Cross recommends that a family of four have the following items in a first-aid kit:

- 2 absorbent compress dressings (5 by 9 inches)
- 25 adhesive bandages (assorted sizes)
- 1 adhesive cloth tape (10 yards by 1 inch)
- 5 antibiotic ointment packets (approximately 1 gram each)
- 5 antiseptic wipe packets
- 2 packets of aspirin (81 mg each)

◈ 1 blanket (space blanket)
◈ 1 breathing barrier (with one-way valve)
◈ 1 instant cold compress
◈ 2 pair of non-latex gloves (size: large)
◈ 2 hydrocortisone ointment packets (approximately 1 gram each)
◈ scissors
◈ 1 roller bandage (3 inches wide)
◈ 1 roller bandage (4 inches wide)
◈ 5 sterile gauze pads (3 by 3 inches)
◈ 5 sterile gauze pads (4 by 4 inches)
◈ oral thermometer (non-mercury/non-glass)
◈ 2 triangular bandages
◈ tweezers
◈ first-aid instruction booklet

As first-aid supplies are used, they should be replaced in order to be ready for the next incident.

For this activity, inventory your family's first-aid kit and see if it is fully equipped. Make a list of any missing items and arrange to restock.

CHRONOLOGY

725–675 B.C.—Greek epic poems the *Iliad* and the *Odyssey*, attributed to the poet Homer, were composed.

640–546 B.C.—Thales, the first Greek natural philosopher, suggested that water was the original substance and that earthquakes had natural causes.

493–433 B.C.—Empedocles, the natural philosopher who proposed four elements: earth, air, fire, and water.

460 B.C.—Traditional birth year of Hippocrates.

430 B.C.—Setting of Plato's dialog *Protagoras* that mentions Hippocrates of Cos.

430–330 B.C.—Most Hippocratic texts written.

427–347 B.C.—Plato, the philosopher who founded the Academy, mentioned Hippocrates, the Asclepiad from Cos, in his dialogues.

384–322 B.C.—Aristotle, philosopher and scientist. In his studies of animals, Aristotle conducts and writes about the first known Greek dissections of animals.

380 B.C.—Often stated as date of Hippocrates' death. Plato founds the Academy in Athens.

300 B.C.—Construction begins on Asclepion of
Cos, a healing sanctuary dedicated to the
hero god Asclepius.

280 B.C.—Museum and library founded in
Alexandria, Egypt. Medical school there
established within a few years.

250 B.C.—First evidence that Hippocratic texts
were studied in Alexandria.

A.D. 1–99—First extant mention of the *Hippocratic
Oath* in other sources.

130–200—Galen of Pergamum. Galen idealized
Hippocrates. Through dissections of
animals, Galen made great strides in
understanding anatomy.

300–399—First extant references to physicians
pledging the *Hippocratic Oath*.

1526—First printed editions of complete works of
Hippocrates published in Venice, Italy.

CHAPTER NOTES

Chapter 1. "The Divine Hippocrates"

1. G. E. R. Lloyd, ed., *Hippocratic Writings* (London: Penguin Books, 1978), p. 67.

2. Ibid., p. 207.

3. Ibid., p. 210.

4. Ibid., pp. 108–109.

5. Ibid., p. 9.

6. P. M. Fraser, *Ptolemaic Alexandria* (Oxford: Clarendon Press, 1972), p. 365.

7. Susan Sherwin-White, *Ancient Cos: A Historical Study From the Dorian Settlement to the Imperial Period* (Gottingen: Vandenhoek & Ruprecht, 1978), p. 38.

8. James Longrigg, *Greek Medicine From the Heroic to the Hellenistic Age* (New York: Routledge, 1998), p. 39.

9. Owsei Temkin, *Hippocrates in a World of Pagans and Christians* (Baltimore: Johns Hopkins Press, 1991), p. 51.

10. Ibid., p. 57.

11. Vivian Nutton, *Ancient Medicine* (New York: Routledge, 2004), pp. 53–54.

12. Temkin, p. 71.

13. Ibid., p. 41.

14. Ibid., p. 49.

15. Longrigg, p. 49.

16. *Dictionary of Scientific Biography*, s.v. "Hippocrates of Cos."

Chapter 2. World of the Hippocratics

1. John Boardman, Jasper Griffin, and Oswyn Murray, eds., *The Oxford History of the Classical World* (Oxford: Oxford University Press, 1986), p. 127.

2. Ibid., p. 212.

3. G. E. R. Lloyd, *Early Greek Science: Thales to Aristotle* (New York: W.W. Norton & Co., 1970), p. 8.

4. James Longrigg, *Greek Medicine From the Heroic to the Hellenistic Age* (New York: Routledge, 1998), p. 19.

5. Lloyd, pp. 17–18.

6. Ibid., p. 42.

Chapter 3. Earlier Medicine

1. Homer, *Iliad,* trans. Robert Fagles (New York: Viking, 1990), 1.11.

2. Ibid., 1.59–60.

3. Ibid., 1.370–372.

4. Ibid., 16.605–611.

5. Ibid., 16.621.

6. Ibid., 11.606–607.

7. P. M. Fraser, *Ptolemaic Alexandria* (Oxford: Clarendon Press, 1972), p. 256.

8. Homer, *Iliad,* 4.240–252.

9. Homer, *Odyssey,* trans. Robert Fagles (New York: Viking, 1996), 19.520.

10. G. E. R. Lloyd, ed., *Hippocratic Writings* (London: Penguin Books, 1978), p. 13.

11. Susan Sherwin-White, *Ancient Cos: A Historical Study From the Dorian Settlement to Imperial Period* (Gottingen: Vandenhoek & Ruprecht, 1978), p. 259.

12. James Longrigg, *Greek Medicine From the Heroic to the Hellenistic Age* (New York: Routledge, 1998), p. 14.

13. Sherwin-White, p. 259.

14. Ibid., p. 261.

15. Lloyd, p. 14.

16. Robert B. Strassler, ed., *The Landmark Herodotus: The Histories* (New York: Pantheon Books, 2007), 3.131.

17. Ibid., 3.131–132.
18. Ibid., 3.129–130.
19. Ibid., 3.130–131.

Chapter 4. Hippocrates of Cos

1. G. E. R. Lloyd, ed., *Hippocratic Writings* (London: Penguin Books, 1978), p. 9.

2. Catherine B. Avery, ed., *The New Century Classical Handbook* (New York: Appleton-Century-Crofts, 1962), p. 489.

3. Vivian Nutton, *Ancient Medicine* (New York: Routledge, 2004), p. 221.

4. Plato, *The Collected Dialogues of Plato,* ed. Edith Hamilton and Huntington Cairns (Princeton: Princeton University Press, 1961), p. 310 (Protagoras 311 b–c).

5. Ibid., p. 516 (Phaedrus 270 c–d).

6. Aristotle *Politics* VII 1326a 15–16.

7. Robert B. Strassler, ed., *The Landmark Thucydides* (New York: Touchstone, 1996), 8:412.

8. Susan Sherwin-White, *Ancient Cos: A Historical Study From the Dorian Settlement to Imperial Period* (Gottingen: Vandenhoek & Ruprecht, 1978), p. 32.

9. Ibid., pp 35–36.

10. Ibid., p. 35.

11. Ibid., p. 261.

12. Ibid., p. 262.

Chapter 5. Science of Medicine

1. G. E. R. Lloyd, ed., *Hippocratic Writings* (London: Penguin Books, 1978), p. 42.

2. Ibid., p. 30.

3. Sherwin B. Nuland, *Doctors: The Biography of Medicine* (New York: Vintage Books, 1988), p. 14.

4. Lloyd, pp. 170–171.

5. Nuland, p. 14.

6. Lloyd, p. 118.

7. Ibid., pp. 106–107.

8. Ibid., p. 237.

9. Ibid.

10. Ibid., p. 248.

11. Ibid., 240.

12. Vivian Nutton, *Ancient Medicine* (New York: Routledge, 2004), p. 119.

13. Ibid., pp. 120–121.

14. George Sarton, *A History of Science: Ancient Science Through the Golden Age of Greece* (Cambridge: Harvard University Press, 1952), p. 339.

15. Vivian Nutton, "Humorialism," *Companion Encyclopedia of the History of Medicine* (New York: Routledge, 1993), vol. 1, p. 281.

16. Ibid., p. 284.

17. Ibid.

18. Nuland, p. 13.

19. Ibid.

20. Nutton, "Humorialism," pp. 286–287.

Chapter 6. The Art of Medicine

1. Hippocrates, *The Genuine Works of Hippocrates,* trans. Francis Adams (Baltimore: Williams & Wilkkins Co., 1939), p. 292.

2. Sherwin B. Nuland, *Doctors: The Biography of Medicine* (New York: Vintage Books, 1988), p. 12.

3. Ibid., p. 15.

4. G. E. R. Lloyd, ed., *Hippocratic Writings* (London: Penguin Books, 1978), p. 170.

5. Ibid., p. 171.

6. Ibid., p. 172.

7. Ibid., p. 177.

8. Ibid., pp. 181–182.

9. Ibid., p. 185.

10. Ibid., p. 188.

11. Ibid.

12. Hippocrates, p. 192.

13. Ibid., pp. 206–207.

14. Ibid., p. 266.

Chapter 7. The Oath

1. James Longrigg, *Greek Medicine From the Heroic to the Hellenistic Age* (New York: Routledge, 1998), p. 106.

2. Owsei Temkin, *Hippocrates in a World of Pagans and Christians* (Baltimore: Johns Hopkins Press, 1991), p. 21.

3. Robert Baker, "The History of Medical Ethics," *Companion Encyclopedia of the History of Medicine* (New York: Routledge, 1993), vol. 1, p. 853.

4. Vivian Nutton, *Ancient Medicine* (New York: Routledge, 2004), p. 69.

5. Ludwig Edelstein, *Ancient Medicine* (Baltimore: The Johns Hopkins University Press, 1967), p. 11.

6. Nutton, p. 68.

7. Howard Markel, "History of Medicine: On the Hippocratic Oath," *Science Week*, 2004, <http://scienceweek.com/2004/sa040917-6.htm> (November 28, 2008).

8. Ibid.

9. Ibid.

10. G. E. R. Lloyd, ed., *Hippocratic Writings* (London: Penguin Books, 1978), p. 67.

Chapter 8. The Ideal Physician

1. Susan Sherwin-White, *Ancient Cos: A Historical Study From the Dorian Settlement to Imperial Period* (Gottingen: Vandenhoek & Ruprecht, 1978), p. 338.

2. Ibid., p. 342.

3. Vivian Nutton, *Ancient Medicine* (New York: Routledge, 2004), p. 109.

4. John T. Bunn, "Origin of the Caduceus Motif," *Journal of the American Medical Society*, vol. 202, no. 7, November 13, 1967.

5. Sherwin-White, p. 264.

6. P. M. Fraser, *Ptolemaic Alexandria* (Oxford: Clarendon Press, 1972), p. 345.

7. Ibid.

8. Nutton, p. 232.

9. Ibid., p. 310.

10. G. E. R. Lloyd, ed., *Hippocratic Writings* (London: Penguin Books, 1978), p. 57.

11. Nutton, p. 60.

GLOSSARY

agora—Marketplace and community center in ancient Greek cities.

anatomy—The science of the bodily structure of living things, including the human body.

aphorism—A short statement of a principle or general truth.

confederacy—A league or alliance for mutual support or common action.

covenant—An agreement, or promise to perform some action.

dissection—The process of disassembling or cutting open something, such as a body, to study its internal structure.

empirical—Based on observation or experiment, not on theory.

epilepsy—A neurological disorder marked by abnormal electrical discharges in the brain.

humors—Four human body fluids: phlegm, blood, black bile, yellow bile.

incantation—Spells or verbal charms spoken in a ritual of magic.

koinon—An ancient Greek guild or trade group; an association for a common goal.

Museum—Sanctuary of the Muses, goddesses of arts and sciences. The famed Museum in Alexandria, Egypt, was a center of study and research.

nausea—Stomach distress with distaste for food; urge to vomit.

papyrus—A paperlike writing material made from the papyrus plant, a reed that grows in Egypt.

peroration—The concluding part of a speech.

phenomena—Observable facts or events, often of scientific interest.

phlegm—Mucus and other materials produced by the lining of the respiratory tract. One of the four humors.

plague—Widespread disease killing many people.

pleurisy—Inflammation of tissues around the lungs.

pneumonia—Inflammation or infection of the lungs.

polis—A Greek city-state.

preamble—An introductory statement in a speech or document.

prognosis—In medicine, the art of foretelling the course of a disease.

pseudepigraphy—Falsely inscribed. Documents once considered to be of historic value that are really fiction.

regimen—In medicine, diet, exercise, and therapy to maintain or improve health.

respiratory—Having to do with breathing.

stethoscope—A medical instrument for detecting sounds inside the body.

symptom—Something that indicates the presence of a bodily disorder.

talent—Unit of weight, often of silver, used as money by ancient Greeks.

FURTHER READING

Books

Dargie, Richard. *Ancient Greece Health and Disease*. Minneapolis, Minn.: Compass Point Books, 2006.

Dawson, Ian. *Greek and Roman Medicine*. New York: Enchanted Lion Books, 2005.

Nardo, Don. *Ancient Greece*. Detroit: Lucent Books, 2006.

Powell, Dr. Anton. *Ancient Greece*. New York: Chelsea House, 2007.

Whiting, Jim. *The Life and Times of Hippocrates*. Hockessin, Del.: Mitchell Lane Publishers, 2006.

Internet Addresses

"Hippocrates," University of Virginia Health System
http://www.hsl.virginia.edu/historical/artifacts/antiqua/hippocrates.cfm

"Works by Hippocrates," The Internet Classics Archive
http://classics.mit.edu/Browse/browse-Hippocrates.html

INDEX